Grace l

Lady of the House

LADY OF THE HOUSE

WRITTEN BY

GRACE R. REYNOLDS

Published by Curious Corvid Publishing

Cover Design by Grace R. Reynolds and Ravven White

Cataloging-in-Publication Data is on file with the Library of Congress.

ISBN: 978-1-7376916-5-5

ISBN (ebook): 978-1-7376916-6-2

www.curiouscorvidpublishing.com

For my husband and daughter,

I love you.

Lady of the House

ACKNOWLEDGMENTS

The creation of this book would not have been possible without the encouragement and support from my friends and family.

I enjoy writing dark poetry, but walking with the character, Lady, was difficult to do at times. I poured some very sad and angry parts of myself into her character and there were days I was irritable because I had chosen her presence as my company. This book does not just tell the fictitious story of the Lady of The House; this book is a work of catharsis that helped me channel emotions that stemmed from some deeply painful experiences in my life into something dark and what I consider to be beautiful.

To my husband, who is very much alive (he asked me to include that bit), thank you for supporting me in my creative writing endeavors, even when it creeps you out most of the time. You are my rock, and you are what keeps me grounded when life feels out of control. I love the man that you are, and I thank you for being an amazing father to our sweet girl.

To my daughter, if you ever read this one day, I hope you will have held on to your ferocious sense of determination and independence. You are the greatest gift that life has given to us, and we are so thankful that you were born into a time where a woman can choose to do and be anything she wants. So dream big baby and shoot for the stars.

For my Instagram Poetry friends, (*you know who you are*) thank you for always expanding my mind to understand and appreciate metaphors in ways I had not been able to before.

To the Curious Corvid in my life, Ravven White, I want to thank you for being my sister in darkness and sounding board. You were one of the first that I shared my idea for this collection with and your encouragement for me to see it through mattered so much. I hope everyone that has read your work or will read your work in the future sees you for the gem that you are. Cheers to us and where our paths in writing will lead.

To my editor, Kindra Austin, thank you for being a part of this journey with the Lady and me. Since I first learned of you, I have admired you as a writer and felt that you were one of the first out there to truly understand my expression through writing, as well as the central emotion that I commonly write through. In many ways I view you as a mentor to myself as a dark writer of poetry.

And finally, thank you dear reader. I hope that your walk with me and the Lady of the House is a cathartic journey for you, too. Don't ever let your grief or anger fester inside of you, for it will eat you alive. Let it die, and let it rise.

Sincerely,

Grace R. Reynolds

INTRODUCTION

I want you to think for a moment about your greatest fear. I want you to imagine telling me why you have let that fear psychologically cripple some aspect of your life. How have you trapped yourself like a bird in a cage when the door is wide open? Now tell me who or what it is that you are using as an excuse to convince yourself that the door is locked shut.

Trauma, in its multiple forms, is an unfortunate reality of the human experience. We can label it to understand it, live with it, and perhaps even cure it. We can also ignore it, repress it, and let it take root inside our bodies until it putrefies us from the inside out.

This book shares the tale of Lady, a 1940s riveter turned housewife trapped by a loveless marriage and societal framework that makes it difficult for her to abandon her current circumstances. She feels purposeless, hopeless, and she is angry. *Resentful.*

And she *festers.*

When writing this book, I poured the emotions I personally felt that stemmed from my own emotional trauma into the character of the Lady. I sought to understand her motivations, frustrations, and learn what it was that she wanted to share with the world. I baked it into a sweet apple pie, made from entrails and gouged out eyes, and wrapped it up in a pretty bow.

This book may excite or repulse you with its macabre imagery, but don't let that distract you from what's simmering beneath its surface. Readers of this book will find an examination of my character's mental well-being. They will learn what happens in a worst-case scenario when suppressed feelings are torn open like a gaping wound, suppurating with pus, and become infected. And they will bear witness to, perhaps, misplaced malice.

Tell me, what do you think would happen if you were to let yourself become infected by your agony and malice? That is what I want you to think about while reading this book. I hope you enjoy your time within the pages of the "Lady of the House." She is an excellent host.

—Grace R. Reynolds

July 2021

TABLE OF CONTENTS

PART I: RESENT

Lady of The House......1

The Autumn of 1945......3

80/20......5

Wither......7

The Latest Fashion......9

Advertisements......11

Lemon Wedge & Sun Tea......13

Calloused Love......15

Intentions......17

An Apology: to Stained Sheets and Smells That Won't Wash Out......19

The Umbra......21

Chicken Noodle Soup......23

Morning Routine......25

Stacking Dishes......27

Bitter Roast......29

Mercy......31

Underneath It All......33

Cabernet......35

Soap Chips......37

Coconut Cream Pie......39

The Skein...41

The Hangover...43

She Writes..45

Sherbet Delight...47

Time Sheets..51

Wick..53

Fuji Automatic 35...55

Clumps..57

Nickel Finish...59

PART II: DESCENT

Nightmare...65

Princess Cut..67

Ambrosia...69

Sunday Drives...71

Ethereal Glow...73

Halitosis..75

Baked Chicken Breasts...77

Edges..79

Q-Tip Knowledge..81

Smile...83

Bloody Valentine...85

Groundswell..87

Italian Wedding Soup...89

Needle...91

Lucky Strike 93

Banister 95

River Skins 97

The Haze 99

Hollow 101

What She Wants 103

Cutlery Knives 105

Iron-Pressed 107

Accessory to Pleasure 109

Ambiguous Loss 111

Sombre Silence 113

PART III: CONTENT

Upholstery Cleaner 117

Melodies of Pain 119

First Snow 121

Dead Calm 123

Cadaver 125

Glass Jar 127

Dirt 129

The Haunting 131

Mirrors 133

Kindling 135

Widow 137

All That Remains 139

Lady of the House

Grace R. Reynolds

LADY OF THE

HOUSE

Lady of the House

Part I: Resent

Lady of the House

LADY OF THE HOUSE

Iridescent oily suds,

Hoary with foam that sops against dishes

Splattered with crusted oregano and tomatoes,

Deep maroon, like how she had imagined

Her hand reaching into the dark abysm

Of the shredder ring openings

In the General Electric garbage disposal unit.

She muffled her cries to suppress the filthy mess

Spewing from her soul, fetid with the hope

That she could be rid of the lingering feeling

That her life was only but a broken promise

Plated in yellow gold that readily reminded her

Of vows she had taken, to learn how to absently gleam

And become endlessly forgiving

As all wives were expected to do,

For it was their job-- their duty--

And after all, *she was* The Lady of The House.

THE AUTUMN OF 1945

The relentless waves of men roiled in with the tide,
Salty with trauma, ready to resume their former lives.
But what about the women who answered
The call to war heavy in mechanics
And munition ready to ship to foreign shores?

Their independence drowned,
By the likes of The Man of Her House,
Eroding like fossils, suppressed deep underground,
Out of which her resentment would sprout and bloom,
Towards her ragged, tired, and unassuming groom.

Lady of the House

80/20

Mother told her on their wedding day that

"a relationship will only satisfy you

eighty percent of the time."

She wondered then, what must it mean

For the remaining twenty percent in between?

Lady of the House

WITHER

The morning dew
Hovers upon blades of grass
Green with envy.

Of nuptials
As dull as wilting carnations –
She withers in the cockcrow hour.

How does a life look
Through the magnified view of tears
Wallowing in the depths of subterranean sorrow?

Feral, white
And rooted in despondence
Now blackened with rot,

Where earthworms
Salivate over dross
To spring forth

A rose.

THE LATEST FASHION

Rusted reveries
Drip in factory grade overalls soiled with
The sweaty satisfaction of a hard day's work,
Steeled with purpose beguiled.

The steam fogs her memories
With hot breath to hide pensive and sinister tears,
Lost in a daydream longing for who she was
For the last two years.

Lady of the House

ᴀDVERTISEMENTS

"HELP WANTED: Secretarial Services"

She showed him the notice in the local paper

And though it wasn't her forte,

She could work because she *had* worked.

He glanced at the headline and met her gaze

"That's hardly worth your time. It's not very good pay."

The ink bled in the palms of her hands

As the perspiration of her anger blotted the paper,

And maybe it would have been less significant

If this was the first time, but it wasn't and she knew that.

It would continue to be a war of the words

Waged in type-form via advertisements.

Lady of the House

LEMON WEDGE & SUN TEA

INGREDIENTS:

- ✔ *6-8 tea bags*
- ✔ *1 lemon, cut into wedges*

DIRECTIONS:

- ✔ *Place tea bags in a gallon glass pitcher*
- ✔ *Cap and place in direct sunlight for 4-6 hours*
- ✔ *When desired strength is achieved, store in refrigerator*
- ✔ *Serve with a fresh wedge of lemon*

Perhaps this weekend

She would kindly ask him to cut the lawn,

And offer to make him some sun tea,

Then plop in three ice cubes, happily.

A snazzy straw would do so nice,

Paired with a lemon wedge to make it look *just right,*

And watch him strain against the old push mower

While her mind begged for him to go slower;

Slower the grind of grassy green blades

Down to the bone.

And who would have known

That the accidental slice

Of his toes could gush such luscious displays

Of envious red hues?

She'd readily come to his aid and squeeze citrus

Over his gaping wounds,

"There, there" she'd smile,

Dead in the eyes keeping her rage at bay,

And he'd grimace perfectly

With a compliment, and say,

"Hey, honey, *this tea tastes great!*"

CALLOUSED LOVE

His hands, rough and calloused,

Wrought with pain and selflessness

Peeled a cuticle back

With dead skin hanging defenseless,

And the cool sting of her touch considered

For a moment

If she ought to pull it back more

To create the perfect spiral,

An effort she had silently acknowledged, was so vile.

He reached out to meet her touch

In a moment

Of lust-filled desperation,

But she pulled back

With anxious frustration,

Not ready to heal

Their calloused love

By means of crusty cambium flirtation.

Were it not her desire

To find intimacy in the heat of a weapons depot,

She might have been able

To unleash her arsenal of bullets, cocked by a libido

That no longer stirred for her partner

Who saw the signs she so desperately tried not to show.

INTENTIONS

Would you have moved for me

As I once moved for you?

Or do you only enjoy my company

For the attention?

Did you like it when I listened

And professed validation for you?

I struggle now to understand

What, exactly, your intentions were.

Lady of the House

Grace R. Reynolds

An Apology: to Stained Sheets and Smells That Won't Wash Out

I can't get you out
No matter how hard I scrub:
The smell of pennies.

Dead lavender crumbs
And ground up rosemary leaves
Cannot mask crimson pools.

What if I told you
These delights were born from pain?
Would you forgive me?

I'll never be clean.
My horrors woven in threads,

19

Stained sheets where love is dead.

THE UMBRA

She wallowed in murky waves of despondence,

Browned by food particles that pull her under

Into the umbra, so muddy and rancid;

The smell of meat wafts up her nose

To consume her thoughts and swallow her whole.

Lady of the House

CHICKEN NOODLE SOUP

INGREDIENTS:

- ✔ Shredded rotisserie chicken
- ✔ 1 chopped onion
- ✔ 2 stalks of chopped celery
- ✔ 2 chopped carrots
- ✔ 1 minced clove of garlic
- ✔ 16 oz of chicken stock
- ✔ 1 package of egg noodles
- ✔ 1 tbsp of butter

DIRECTIONS:

- ✔ Heat butter in large pot over medium heat
- ✔ Add minced garlic and cook for 1 minute
- ✔ Add chopped vegetables until onions are translucent
- ✔ Add chick stock and bring to boil. Cook until vegetables become tender.
- ✔ Add shredded chicken and egg noodles until noodles are cooked through.
- ✔ Add salt and pepper for taste

An onion-stained butcher's block

Crafted from maple and the scars

Of one thousand knives

Minced the vegetables, finally.

The celery and carrots mocked her with hues

Of muted green envy and tangerine

As she labored over chicken noodle soup

For a life so mundanely obscene.

Wait, did she move over the clothes

In the washing machine?

If she would just keep chopping

Maybe one of these days, she would finally cut

The tips of her fingers enough

For her to feel the sting and watch them bleed

To remember that she could still feel something.

MORNING ROUTINE

0530: Wake up, get dressed, prepare your hair, and make sure no strands are out of place.

0545: Wipe moisturizer on your face, hurry, or his breakfast will be late!

0600: No time to waste, throw back the curtains. He'll probably want bacon, this you're certain.

0630: Serve the breakfast, serve the coffee. Pull the juice from the refrigerator   and hand him his favorite newspaper.

0700: Wave goodbye, clean up the kitchen. Don't stop moving or you'll have to listen to idle thoughts routinely suppressed,

Keep moving dear, you're not allowed to be stressed!

STACKING DISHES

How she wished

He would accidentally slip

On a puddle, so wet, from stacking dishes,

That he'd fall onto a knife,

An excuse to evade supper together for the night.

Lady of the House

BITTER ROAST

Coffee warm, but company silent,

She stirs the creamer round and round

Until he coughs, and for a moment she wonders

If this morning's conversation will be more substantive

Than the advertisement in the paper.

"How attractive are you?" it reads,

As if that isn't insulting enough, it beckons

Her eyes search for the answers on how to gain

The curves men so desperately crave—

As if she had someone to impress

Forgetting about the man

Sitting across the table from her.

He says goodbye and hurries out the door, and like the

Instant caffeinated rush her beverage provided,

She felt the guilt; the shame of not being enough
Because she didn't want to be enough,
And she wasn't.

MERCY

Her mother used to wring washrags

Every night, twisting and turning the damp cloth

Tighter and tighter until it was dry.

She used to watch her squeeze that dirty water out,

Compressing it until there was no room left for

Droplets to exist.

She held her stomach that afternoon

And thought of that moment.

Her insides pulsated with brilliant pain

As she checked the napkin dabbed between her legs.

A crimson cross that bled with mixed feelings

Of joy, anxiety, and relief proved to her

That God had shown her mercy

And she thanked Him for the bleeding.

Underneath It All

Rosy blemishes

Freckle along her chin and cheeks,

Inflamed with the fear that the pinkish pale powder

Will hide the brute that she is underneath.

A dash of rouge and eye shadow,

Perfectly matched to her robin egg blue sweater

To make her eyes sparkle like diamonds,

A girl's best friend, the kind that comes

In the form of a porcelain doll

Handpicked from the storefront display

To be the perfect companion,

But every toy has some type of defect

And she was cracking all over.

Lady of the House

CABERNET

Dinner parties were never her forte,

But The Man of the House wanted it that way--

Meetings with friends or businessmen,

Around the table framed by her mother's fine china,

And glasses filled with Cabernet.

Would this be it?

A future dimly lit by crystals shimmering

Against brushed gold,

Casting shadows against the polished silver

And the wine glasses that they would hold?

She looked into the abysm of her fill

And thought to herself that this was hell,

Forever making her out to be just a pretty face

Set against expensive plates

And inherited cutlery.

Lady of the House

SOAP CHIPS

The separation of colors and whites

From hand-washed linens

Forced her to confront the dirtiest stain

She had ever seen:

The outline of crimson lips on his collar,

Conspicuously thrown in the hamper

Haphazardly, as if he weren't trying to hide

His paramour.

The trauma of a life wasted,

Built on a foundation of suburban lawns

With pinwheels spinning in calm winds.

Her mind wanders to a time

When he used to steal kisses

Under high school bleachers,

Where he would leave hickeys on her neck;

His own imprint.

Impulsively,

She throws the blouse away

And decides to pour just a little bit

Of laundry detergent

In his cereal

The following morning.

COCONUT CREAM PIE

INGREDIENTS:

- ✔ 2/3 cups sugar
- ✔ ½ cup of flour
- ✔ ¼ teaspoon salt
- ✔ 2 egg yolks
- ✔ 2 cups milk
- ✔ 9-inch pie shell
- ✔ 1 cup toasted shredded coconut
- ✔ 1 tsp. Vanilla extract

DIRECTIONS:

- ✔ Mix sugar, salt, and flour in the top of a double boiler pan
- ✔ In a separate bowl, combine egg yolks with milk
- ✔ Stir wet ingredients into dry until they are blended
- ✔ Cook over hot water until the mixture thickens
- ✔ Cover and cook for ten more minutes
- ✔ Add vanilla extract and pour into pie shell
- ✔ Let the mixture cool
- ✔ Before serving, add whipped cream and toasted coconut on top

What do you do when your husband calls you

early in the day

To excitedly tell you that he got a raise

At the company you used to work at?

The one that sent you packing

To open up a space for men, like him,

Only to realize how easily you could be replaced?

You bake him a god damn pie,

Slap a smile on your face,

And let yourself die a little inside.

T̶HE S̶KEIN

The black rotary phone

Rings incessantly, he answers aggressively,

And she wonders why he even pretends

To hide his extramarital reveries,

But he pretends to demand

They don't call 'round there anymore.

"Just a telemarketer, nothing more."

She nods and knits mittens for a baby that isn't there,

Not like he actually cares.

She weaves the yarn and wonders what it would be like,

If the needles were twined within his entrails,

What a marvelous ombré that skein would be,

Red, red, and even more red.

Lady of the House

THE HANGOVER

She inspects the stagnant pond

Of purples and reds; she swirls it by the stem,

Churning her view of the life she lives, once so secure,

But now hangs in the balance between her fingertips,

Each one leaving their own imprint,

Foggy, like little clouds masking

Swampy crimson lust and deceit.

She drinks one glass, then two, then three

Until her mind is a hazy dream of plummy currents

Running through river beds of crusted lipstick stains

To bleed across glassy reflections that unveil

The clarity of the hangover.

Lady of the House

Grace R. Reynolds

SHE WRITES

You say I am not

A bird trapped in a cage,

But you were the one who clipped my wings.

Lady of the House

SHERBET DELIGHT

INGREDIENTS:

- ✔ 12 oz evaporated milk
- ✔ 6 oz frozen orange juice concentrate
- ✔ ½ cup sugar
- ✔ ¼ tsp salt

DIRECTIONS:

- ✔ Open and freeze milk until ice forms around edges
- ✔ Combine remaining ingredients in a bowl
- ✔ Add iced milk into chilled mixing bowl.
- ✔ Add the remaining ingredients slowly, one spoon at a time.
- ✔ Continue to stir until the mixture is very stiff.
- ✔ Pour mixture into freezer tray until it is firm.

A special treat

For a special feast,

The one where she'd tell him

She'd had an interview

For the job, she found in the paper.

He dips his spoon

In the sherbet delight

And thought how the taste tickled his tongue

The way hers used to do in the place

Between his thighs

She tells him the news

And he throws down his spoon.

"What good is a wife

Who only wants to work?

It's like all you want

Is to cause me emotional hurt.

You listen up and you listen clear

Get smart here at home and act more deserving

Of the life I have given you here,

Your house; your *home* –"

"The one where I wallow, all alone."

A pregnant pause

Between the two,

He gathered himself

And left the room.

She reserved her speech,

Traded it for silence,

And silence, sometimes,

Is the crackling spark

For an act of violence.

Lady of the House

TIME SHEETS

She saw her reflection against the dead screen

Playing reels of the news over and over again.

Where was she?

Where were the stories about women like her?

Rising to the occasion only to fall from grace

Like forging time sheets, just to save face.

Lady of the House

WICK

She thought back

To when he left, her eyes welled with tears,

Unsure of his return,

And now she looked at him,

Waiting for his life to end like a wick

Whose wax trickled and trickled and trickled...

What a slow burn.

Lady of the House

Fuji Automatic 35

The Man of the House

Snaps a photo of his blushing bride

With his coveted Fuji Automatic 35.

He thought of better days gone by,

When their love was budding and brand new.

But something between them has inherently changed,

And he's started to wonder if his wife will stay sane,

So he does what all men of his era feel they must do:

Fix what is broken and get on to something new.

CLUMPS

Devoid of all emotions,

She clutched her legs

As she sat at the bottom of the shower

To watch the hair that she had pulled

Clump atop the drain.

Lady of the House

Grace R. Reynolds

NICKEL FINISH

I often wonder why

The warm water feels colder

When I sit down in the bottom

Of the shower, as if the farther away I am

From the head it loses its heat. So I turn

The knob left to feel it singe against

My back, knowing that it will

Make me woozy. I sit

there and feel my flesh

Burn like fire, just

Enough to become

Numb and I

Watch the

Drain

Swallow

The

Water

That

Swirls

59

And

Swirls

And

Swirls around

The nickel finish

And wonder if it's

Taking the

Parts of

Me

I

Am

Trying

To shed.

The sin of my

Skin that I want to

Scrub away with lavender

And oatmeal. My hair waterfalls

Over my face and through its curtain

I continue to watch the drain slurp down my

Essence into the abysm below and I can feel my

Heart lodge itself in the globs of soap and hair that

Line cast iron... but water is persistent and finds a

Way through every crevice to seep through the

Sludge that is home to the flies, silverfish,

And the centipedes. It is here, down

Below where I feel I can look up to

A sky that pours in with light

Through the strainer and

From what I can see

It looks beautiful

From down

Here. It's

Like

there

Is

Still

Hope.

Lady of the House

bod ( ).

Grace R. Reynolds

PART II:

DESCENT

Lady of the House

NIGHTMARE

I keep having this dream
Where I'm floating
In an infinity pool
Of black sludge
Where I am
Sleeping.
Is this
Real?
"No.
You are
Only dreaming"
Is what the voice says
And it's so calming to hear
Because I'm so trusting of the fact
That nothing can hurt me while I lay on my back
With my heart towards a sky of emptiness, a void
That cannot be filled with happy memories or
Times of grief or anger, it is only here that
I feel completely emptied out of the
Black gunk that clogs up my
Drains and leaves my
Hands covered in
Questionable
Things like
Eyebrow
Hair and
There are
Hands under me

Stroking my back but I
Can't move or shout and my
Eyes are still shut but oh god I can
Feel it pushing into my muscles and it's
Outlining the vertebrae in my spinal column,
Help me please, get me out of here I can't bear it
It keeps pressing and gripping I can't fight it and if I
Open my eyes I know it will see me and it will feel
My back stiffen and my heart pump with fury as
I try to break free of its grasp only for it to
Pull me under and break my back
Why did I ever think I would be
Safe here in the confines
Of my mind, if I could
Just wake up I'll
Be just fine.

PRINCESS CUT

The desecration of a marriage,

Pulverized by the razor edges of a diamond,

Princess cut and audaciously insolent,

Dazzling in the supernova,

Of broken promises,

And skin flayed eyelids,

His irises, the nebula's center.

AMBROSIA

INGREDIENTS:

- ✔ ¾ cup heavy cream chilled
- ✔ ¼ cup powdered sugar
- ✔ 1/2 teaspoon vanilla extract
- ✔ ½ cup sour cream
- ✔ 4 cups of mini marshmallows
- ✔ 1 eye from the person that betrayed you
- ✔ 1 ½ cups sweetened shredded coconut
- ✔ 1 can of mandarin oranges
- ✔ ½ cup maraschino cherries stems removed
- ✔ 1 cup chopped pineapple

DIRECTIONS:

- ✔ Mix cream and sugar until stiff peaks are formed.
- ✔ Add sour cream
- ✔ Add marshmallows, orange, pineapple, coconut, and cherries
- ✔ Stir to combine
- ✔ Top with the eye of a treacherous soul
- ✔ Transfer to a glass serving bowl,
- ✔ Refrigerate 2 hours before serving

In butter-colored Pyrex

She delicately places candied cherries,

Deliciously sweet and almost tart

To the touch of the tongue,

And yet she is dissatisfied

Because she wishes they were her husband's eyes

With optic nerves flayed like sticky confetti streams

Lacquered in thick crimson syrup

Dripping over tangy oranges and pineapples,

And cushioned with marshmallows and heavy cream

It would all be so perfect

Because presentation is everything.

SUNDAY DRIVES

Eyelids ascendant and fixed upon the crucifix

Emaciated, strung up with poking ribs;

The Son of God.

For a moment she wondered

If redemption's drops prickled upon

Her crown of thorns; she signs the cross

Only to find her fingers revealed: nothing.

Perhaps another time.

They bid goodbyes to the Father

With donuts and coffee in hand

For their habitual Sunday drive.

Her visions swirl like exhaust fume clouds

From their vehicle destroyed at the bottom of a ravine,

Her signature robin blue dress, blood splattered

And her husband's jacket tattered

Exposing his wet spleen.

She searches for their reflections

In dull guard rails sheen.

ETHEREAL GLOW

1959 never looked so fine,

Illuminated by the fluorescent blue light,

Humming the sounds of nostalgic summer nights,

Where hungry mosquitoes and buzzing flies

Hovered in the ethereal glow.

Were they searching for a higher truth

While monotonously drumming their wings

Against fragile exoskeletons?

If they could just touch God, maybe they would know...

Her husband laughs as their lives end

In disappointing zaps.

Lady of the House

Grace R. Reynolds

HALITOSIS

A wave of hot breath

Tastes stale and smells like fresh death...

He says good morning.

With every yawn she imagined

Animal droppings tumbling

And hag moths fluttering

From his rotten mandible that she has yet to gut out.

Lady of the House

BAKED CHICKEN BREASTS

INGREDIENTS:

- ✔ *4 boneless skinless chicken breasts*
- ✔ *1 Tablespoon melted butter or olive oil*
- ✔ *1 teaspoon kosher salt*
- ✔ *1/2 teaspoon freshly cracked black pepper*
- ✔ *1/2 teaspoon garlic powder*
- ✔ *1/2 teaspoon paprika*

DIRECTIONS:

- ✔ *Brine chicken in kosher salt*
- ✔ *Heat oven to 450 degrees*
- ✔ *Create mix of spices and olive oil*
- ✔ *Toss chicken in mixture*
- ✔ *Bake for 20 minutes*

The Man of the House

Rubs her diamond shoulders

To compliment her preparation for dinner

"I like the way you massage those breasts!"

He says with a wink

"Just like how I imagine your lungs."

"What's that, hon?"

"Nothing, dear."

EDGES

Do you see that crack?
It's there in the wallpaper
Creeping behind perforated edges
And leaking.

I will peel it back
And break it down to
Reveal the plaster
And finally stop
The bleeding.

Lady of the House

Q-TIP KNOWLEDGE

Her malicious monologue

Reverberates in the drum of her ear;

She inches the Q-tip farther.

> *You could do more;*
>
> *You should be more,*
>
> *But you lay on your belly*
>
> *Trapped, while your husband*
>
> *Screws that whore behind your back,*
>
> *And you just take it.*
>
> *Why do you just take it?*

> *Because if I left*
>
> *I don't think I could make it.*

She takes out the Q-tip

And decides to break it.

Lady of the House

SMILE

"Just smile," he says

So she leans in for a kiss,

Imagining what it would feel like

To chew out his tongue,

But is too afraid to whisper,

"I'm done."

Lady of the House

BLOODY VALENTINE

Let me count the ways

I've dreamt of chewing your hands

To destroy your touch.

GROUNDSWELL

The caving of her psyche,

Like a crater her emotions

Once put together, now asunder,

Was she just broken?

"I am broken."

"I am broken."

"I am broken."

She felt herself slipping,

And was afraid the cup of coffee

Was another glass of wine

Ready to pull her under its scarlet waves

Of morose destruction.

Maybe she just needed another little green pill

To numb her from this existence.

Lady of the House

ITALIAN WEDDING SOUP

INGREDIENTS:

- ✔ ½ pound of ground beef
- ✔ ½ pound of ground pork
- ✔ ½ cup of bread crumbs
- ✔ ¼ cup chopped parsley
- ✔ 1 ½ tsp minced oregano
- ✔ ½ cup finely shredded parmesan
- ✔ 1 large egg
- ✔ Salt and freshly ground black pepper
- ✔ 1 Tbsp olive oil
- ✔ Diced carrots, onion, celery and garlic
- ✔ 14.5 oz of chicken broth
- ✔ ½ pound of fresh spinach

DIRECTIONS:

- ✔ Stir the ingredients in a pot
- ✔ Watch his gaze and hope his eyes rot
- ✔ Add pasta and meatballs to the broth
- ✔ Turn the temperature down to medium-hot
- ✔ Stir occasionally and sprinkle with cheese

The Man of The House

Slurps Italian Wedding Soup

Sip by sip,

Slurp by slurp,

And she watches him

Wishing he would jam that stupid spoon in his eye,

Scoop it out and suck on it until it shriveled up dry.

Needle

A sewing needle

Jammed under her cuticle

Hurts, but not lethal.

Lady of the House

Lucky Strike

Her forlorn figure is trapped

In the afternoon shadow's silhouette,

Framed by the sitting room window;

She slouches with seven sedatives

In her perfectly manicured hands,

Gently pinching her *Lucky Strike*

While her lipstick stains the tipping paper.

The Lady of the House

Wished in that moment

That a truck would come hurtling through

The glass panes to splatter her entrails,

All wrapped up in twenty-six inches

Against the botanical striped wallpaper.

Lady of the House

BANISTER

She runs her clammy palms

Down a splintered banister

Never repaired, it punctures her skin.

Black and blue knuckles

Bruised from punching rusty nails

Hammered deep into

A cracked foundation

That time never healed.

Lady of the House

RIVER SKINS

INGREDIENTS:

- ✔ ¼ salami
- ✔ Crackers
- ✔ Olives
- ✔ Pickles
- ✔ Brie cheese
- ✔ Gruyere cheese
- ✔ Cherries, berries and grapes

DIRECTIONS:

- ✔ Serve ingredients in a visually appealing manner on a large serving platter.
- ✔ Add serving knives and spoons
- ✔ Hope his blood doesn't splatter!

A trip to the store

To shop for ingredients necessary

To create the most appealing charcuterie board.

Funky cheeses paired with nuts, berries

And a little bit of honey.

Should she pick up salami?

Or would she carve away

The skin from her husband's thighs

To make folded rivers on the cutting board display

And garnish it with rosemary or thyme?

The Haze

Blackberries roll on the floor

As his arms are found wrapped in the embrace

Of the woman she always knew was there

But now she was here,

And it was all so clear

How dumb she had let herself be:

The shirt,

The phone calls,

Dumb as a fucking wall,

      And what happened next

      Was something she never dreamed of before:

            V I O L E N T   R A M P A G E

            B L O O D   R E D   H A Z E

Lady of the House

HOLLOW

A creature within
Clawed her way out to save me
From your hollow words.

Lady of the House

WHAT SHE WANTS

"What do you want from me?"

He shrieked, as his head throbbed from being slammed

Against the cabinet door, her eyes no longer hers,

Now a shade of dark carnivore,

"I thought you didn't love me anymore!"

Harpy fueled rage

Guided by fury she sought not to understand –

> *"Your heart in my hands,*
>
> That *is what I want from you."*

Lady of the House

CUTLERY KNIVES

The glint of a blade pulled from the knife block

They had received as a present on their wedding day

Glided towards the Man of the House,

Ready to gut out his organs to splatter and spray—

The Lady of the House

Heard wedding bells ringing in her ears,

And it was the happiest she had felt in years.

Lady of the House

IRON-PRESSED

He tries to shake her in desperation

And cries out with an anguished plea,

But she is no longer listening,

And somehow time has slowed down enough

For her to slice through

His iron-pressed white button-down shirt

So she can watch his blood spurt and bloom

As she watches the demise of her squelching groom.

Lady of the House

ACCESSORY TO PLEASURE

His little paramour

Cowers in the doorway like a dirty bird

Ready to be rinsed of the muddy film along its feathers

Brought on from the petrichor of bloody rain.

The Lady of the House knows better than to turn away

A guest in their home

And treats her with the nicety of pressing

Her perfectly red manicured nails

Into the corners of her eyes to threaten and pop

Her irises out from the immense pressure

To atone for both her and her husband's lies

For she was an accessory to pleasure.

After the puncture and burst

The Lady of the House silently watched that little bird

Collapse into a bath, unable to flutter in her own filth,

And the Lady of the House, like a dutiful spouse,

Genuflected and made the sign of the cross

Across her brow.

AMBIGUOUS LOSS

She stared at him with disbelief, clouded by fibers

Floating around like worms through her point of view,

And like her childhood she had concluded

That she suddenly outgrew him

And was filled with the sensation

Of ambiguous loss.

His heart, now bloody, in the palm of her hands,

Thick with juicy capillaries that led to arteries

And ventricles she thought

She could hear still pumping,

Once flowed with a young love that had fervently beat

Had now been silenced like another cut of meat.

Lady of the House

Somber Silence

Her face had gone numb

While her hands shook and reverberated

As she came down from the adrenaline rush—

Her body writhed and panicked

As gasps escaped from her lips

Parted barely as she stood there

In somber silence.

Lady of the House

Part III:

Content

Lady of the House

UPHOLSTERY CLEANER

She wasn't sure how many days it had been

Since she killed, but the blood stains in the carpet

Were starting to dry and crust,

And no amount of upholstery cleaner

Could remove the filemot of her mortal sin.

Perhaps she would rip up the fibers,

Watch them fray on plastic liner,

Or leave them there to smell

Like the pennies that reeked between

The stitching of her marital bed sheets.

Two bodies, one lie.

Not exactly what she imagined when she pledged

"For better or worse."

Lady of the House

Grace R. Reynolds

MELODIES OF PAIN

The ringling jingling
Of my crimson-stained chainsaw:
Melodies of pain.

FIRST SNOW

Frostbitten feet

Part the red sea of ice crystals and fresh blood,

Plunging forth from the stumpy nape

Of his head, cradled in her hands.

As the snow descends,

Surrounding her in winter's billowing vignette,

She prays it will absorb the sound

Of her screams; the agony of choosing

To finally be alone.

Lady of the House

DEAD CALM

You are my icy fear
Burning with a cold betrayal
Concocted by the curling chaos of your mind.

You are the groundswell of my disgust
Rooted in the comforts of your lies.

My brittle frostbitten fingers
Shatter like jagged glass
Whose cracking sound
Is absorbed by the dismal abyss
Of a beastly winter's howl
That wheezes into a dead calm.

Lady of the House

CADAVER

Here lies a torso

Cradled in a pile of leaves,

Smelling like fresh dirt

Ready to serve as the fertilizer

To a new bed of roses, springing forth from

The dross that was her former life, begotten by

A God that presumed she righteously serve and worship

His patriarchal soliloquy to entrap the daughters of Eve

In holy matrimony to the sons of Adam

That would rebuke their wives for seeking knowledge

That may cause them to question the very fabrication

Of their existence and what it was in that God,

That Man,

They were supposed to believe.

Lady of the House

GLASS JAR

She keeps a glass jar

Full of nail clippings and hair:

Memories of him.

Lady of the House

ⒹIRT

The enduring fortitude of the worm

Squirms through the dirt and into

The decaying folds of flesh,

And a skull, now a warm bowl of cambium requiem

And host for small spiders, pill bugs,

And nicked up wedding bands,

And vermes inched inwards,

Past brain matter and through rotten ear lobes

Masticated by its terrestrial brethren towards a feast

That was the closest thing

To Heaven.

Lady of the House

Grace R. Reynolds

THE HAUNTING

A quiet saunter

Through rooms of peeling paper;

Her mundane haunting.

Lady of the House

MIRRORS

I hope when you think
Of me, you walk past mirrors
That show your decay.

Mirrors that highlight the wretchedness of your soul
Oozing through your bones.

That in reflections
You see a carved hollow place
Where your heart once was.

Lady of the House

KINDLING

I carried your name

On a small piece of paper

And cast it away into the dancing flames,

Forgetting that I once thought

You could be my peace.

Lady of the House

WIDOW

Widow.

Five letters that summarized

Fifteen years of marriage spent

In rose-stained, cheeky smiles

And sticky tacky lipstick lies.

She was now but a husk of his blushing bride.

Widow.

She liked the feel of it

As it whispered between her lips.

The air of it reminded her of a cigarette.

It made her feel calm, cool, collected, and steady.

It made her feel like she was ready

To step back out into the world

No longer as a blushing bride

Or presumed anxiety riddled half-wit.

Widow.

Her hot breath breathed it onto the frosty window.

She kissed the glass,

And grabbed her camel hair long coat.

It was time to start that secretarial job

And see where her new life would go.

Widow.

Widow.

Widow.

As she grabbed for her purse

The Lady of The House was beaming

At how the word 'widow' sounded more like a blessing

Then a curse.

ALL THAT REMAINS

I would use our laughs

As kindling

To stoke the flames

So that I could burn

The memory of you

And all that remains.

Lady of the House

Grace R. Reynolds is a native of the great state of New Jersey, where she was first introduced to the eerie and strange thanks to local urban legends of a devil creeping through the Pine Barrens. Since then, her curiosity with things that go bump in the night bloomed into creative expression as a dark poet, horror, and thriller fiction writer.

When Grace is not writing she can be found dreaming up macabre scenarios inspired by the mundane realities of life. *Lady of The House* is her debut collection of poetry.

Connect with Grace at www.spillinggrace.com or follow her on Instagram @spillinggrace.

Lady of the House

If you or someone you know are struggling with your mental health, please do not hesitate to reach out to someone you trust and seek help. From one human to another, the help is always worth it.

CPSIA information can be obtained
at www.ICGtesting.com
Printed in the USA
BVHW041819151221
624132BV00014B/1258